Photographs help you remember things that happened in the past. That's nice sometimes. But there are some things that people don't want to remember, some things they prefer to keep secret. And if you have photographs of other people's secrets, what do you do with them? Secrets can be bought and sold – especially in the world of horse-racing, where large amounts of money change hands frequently and quickly.

George Millace is a photographer. He is good at taking photographs of other people's secrets, and he has a clever way of hiding his photographs. When he dies suddenly, Philip Nore accidentally finds his hidden photographs. Philip is not only a racehorse rider, but also a good photographer, and he begins to uncover George's photographic secrets. Then he learns that he is not the only person interested in these photographs – but he is the only one who doesn't want to destroy them.

WITHDRAWN

OXFORD BOOKWORMS LIBRARY

Thriller & Adventure

Reflex

Stage 4 (1400 headwords)

Series Editor: Jennifer Bassett
Founder Editor: Tricia Hedge
Activities Editors: Jennifer Bassett and Christine Lindop

DICK FRANCIS

Reflex

Retold by
Rowena Akinyemi

OXFORD UNIVERSITY PRESS

OXFORD
UNIVERSITY PRESS

Great Clarendon Street, Oxford OX2 6DP

Oxford University Press is a department of the University of Oxford.
It furthers the University's objective of excellence in research, scholarship,
and education by publishing worldwide in

Oxford New York

Auckland Cape Town Dar es Salaam Hong Kong Karachi
Kuala Lumpur Madrid Melbourne Mexico City Nairobi
New Delhi Shanghai Taipei Toronto

With offices in

Argentina Austria Brazil Chile Czech Republic France Greece
Guatemala Hungary Italy Japan Poland Portugal Singapore
South Korea Switzerland Thailand Turkey Ukraine Vietnam

OXFORD and OXFORD ENGLISH are registered trade marks of
Oxford University Press in the UK and in certain other countries

Original edition © Dick Francis 1980
First published 1980 by Michael Joseph Ltd
This simplified edition © Oxford University Press 2008
Database right Oxford University Press (maker)
First published in Oxford Bookworms 1991

4 6 8 10 9 7 5 3

ISBN 978 0 19 479182 3

Typeset by Hope Services (Abingdon) Ltd

Printed in Hong Kong

Illustrated by: Dylan Gibson

Word count (main text): 16,500 words

For more information on the Oxford Bookworms Library,
visit www.oup.com/bookworms

CONTENTS

■ ■ ■ ■ ■

1

■ ■ ■ ■ ■

Just another fall

I lay on one elbow, my mouth full of grass and dirt. The horse I'd been riding got to its feet and galloped away. I waited. I was breathing fast, bones aching from the fall. Nothing broken. Just another fall. At the sixteenth fence, the three-mile race, Sandown Park. It was November and it was raining.

I stood up slowly and began to walk back up the hill. I had been riding that horse only because a friend of mine, Steve Millace, who usually rode it, had gone to his father's funeral. What a stupid job for a grown man, I thought. Then I felt surprised with myself. Riding horses was the only job I knew, and I couldn't do it unless I enjoyed it. 'I love it, of course I do,' I told myself.

The only good thing about my fall, I supposed, was that Steve Millace's father had not photographed it. George Millace, famous photographer of the horse-racing world, was by now safe in his box in the ground. Goodbye to George's camera, which was always watching the worst moments, catching the arms in the air, the face in the dirt. George had been a wonderful photographer, but he never showed you winning. He only showed the bad moments.

It seemed strange that we were never going to see

I lay on one elbow, my mouth full of grass and dirt.

George again – his bright, clever eyes, his long nose and moustache, his thin mouth. When Steve had told us about his father's death, the jockeys in the weighing room had not felt sorry.

When I reached the weighing room, the trainer and owner were waiting for me.

'You made a mistake there, Philip, didn't you?' the trainer said, angrily.

I said nothing. The horse was badly trained.

'You're not hurt, are you?' asked the owner.

I shook my head and went into the weighing room. I loved racing, I told myself again. Nothing was wrong except the weather, the fall, the lost race . . . nothing important.

The next day Steve Millace was at Sandown Park. He came into the changing room half an hour before the first race, his hair wet with rain, his eyes angry.

'There was a burglary,' he said, 'at my mother's house yesterday, while we were all out at my father's funeral!'

We sat in rows and listened to him in surprise. I looked at the room. Jockeys were changing into racing clothes and boots, mouths open and eyes turned towards Steve. Automatically I reached for my camera and took a couple of photographs. No one noticed: photography was my hobby, and all the jockeys were used to my camera.

'It was awful,' Steve said. 'Mum had made some cakes and the burglars had thrown them on the walls and floor.

Furniture was broken. Dad's darkroom was destroyed. They took all his photographs. And they took Mum's new coat . . .'

Steve stopped suddenly. It was too much for him. He was twenty-three, a serious person and very fond of his parents. He was small, with bright, dark eyes.

I was going to ride Daylight in a big race that day. Daylight was a good horse and I had a great chance of winning. I usually rode about two races a day, and I didn't win many. Perhaps forty winners a season. I was taller and heavier than the best jockeys – a strong jockey, but not the best. Today, I was almost certain to win, and I was feeling happy.

I finished third in my first race and then prepared to ride Daylight. Daylight's trainer, Harold Osborne, was waiting with the horses.

'You'll lose this race, Philip,' he said quietly.

I smiled. 'I'll try to win.'

'No you won't,' he said sharply. 'Lose it. Victor's money is on another horse.'

I was angry. Victor Briggs owned many of the horses Harold trained. He had done this before, but not for about three years. He came to the races often, but he was secretive and never talked to me much.

Harold Osborne had told me that I must always obey Victor Briggs. I was Harold's jockey and I needed the job. Three years ago, I had lost races for Victor, but I didn't like it and I never took money for it.

'Why don't you take the money?' Harold had said.

I had shaken my head. Probably I was stupid, but somewhere, when I was a child, I had learned to be honest. For three years I had ridden to win, and now the problem appeared again.

'I can't lose,' I argued. 'Daylight's the best horse in the race. You know he is.'

'Lose it,' Harold said. 'And keep quiet.'

I looked at Victor Briggs. He was watching the horses, and pretending not to listen to Harold.

'The money's on another horse,' Harold said. 'Fall off – or come in second. But not first. Understood?'

I understood. I was thirty years old now, and I had been riding Harold's horses for seven years. If I lost my job with Harold, it would be difficult to get another because of my age.

I rode Daylight down to the start. I was angry and miserable. I wanted to win. Daylight was a confident jumper and he fell only occasionally. He was a good horse and I had ridden him many times. Won six races on him.

Cheat the horse. Cheat the people watching. Cheat.

I did it at the third fence, going down the hill. It was a difficult fence. The hill was steep and many horses fell there during the year.

'I'm sorry, boy,' I thought, 'but down you go.'

Daylight hesitated as he jumped. Perhaps he felt my anger. I kicked him at the wrong moment, and pulled at his mouth. I moved forward too far over his shoulder. He landed heavily and his head went down.

The next moment I was off his back. I slid down his neck and fell on to the grass under his feet. Daylight didn't fall. He hesitated, and then galloped after the other horses. In a moment the noise and the horses were gone.

I sat on the quiet ground and took off my helmet, and felt absolutely miserable.

2

Box of rubbish

'Bad luck,' they said in the weighing room.

I felt ashamed and sat down and stared at the floor. I wondered if any of them guessed, but perhaps they didn't.

'Cheer up, Philip,' Steve Millace said. He picked up his helmet. 'There's always another day.'

'Yes.'

He went off to ride and I changed my clothes. The excitement was gone.

I went out to watch the race. Steve drove his horse into the last fence and crashed to the ground. It was a hard fast fall, a fall that broke bones. Steve lay still while his horse got up and galloped away.

I watched as two men helped Steve into an ambulance. A bad day for him as well, I thought, with all his family troubles, too. Why did we do it? Why didn't we sit at a desk in an office? I walked back to the weighing room. My bruises, where Daylight had stepped on me, were beginning to hurt.

Steve came in. His head was bent to one side and his face was white.

'Collar bone,' he said, crossly. 'Could you possibly drive me home? To my mother's house, near Ascot?' He

Steve's head was bent to one side and his face was white.

sounded shy, not sure if I would agree. I saw that his shoulder was hurting badly.

'Yes, all right.' I took a photograph of him.

'What do you do with all those?' he asked.

'Put them in a cupboard.'

Steve looked at the Nikon camera. 'Dad saw some of your pictures. He said that one day you would be a great photographer.'

'He was laughing at me.'

My mother's friend, Charlie, had taught me about photography. My mother had left me with him when I was twelve years old and I had lived with him for three years.

'I can't believe that Dad is gone,' Steve said as we walked out to my car.

'What happened?' I asked. 'You said your Dad drove into a tree.'

'Yes. We think that he went to sleep. There was a bend in the road and he didn't turn. He just drove straight on.' He shook his head. 'He was on his way home from the races at Doncaster and he stopped at a friend's house for a drink. They had a couple of whiskies. It was so stupid.'

We drove a long way without talking, he with his problems and I with mine.

'Turn left here,' Steve said at last.

Suddenly there were lights and people. An ambulance. A police car. People were coming and going from one of the houses.

'Oh no!' said Steve. 'That's my house!'

I parked the car outside the house.

'It's Mum,' Steve said. 'It must be.' His eyes were wide with worry and he looked very young.

'Stay here,' I said. 'I'll go and see.'

Mrs Millace was in the sitting room. I had seen her before: a good-looking, happy woman of fifty. Now she looked terrible. Someone had beaten her. There were cuts on her face and her mouth and nose were bleeding. A policeman was sitting beside her. There was food on the walls, furniture was broken, papers and magazines were thrown all over the floor.

When I walked into the room, the policeman turned his head. 'Are you the doctor?'

'No . . .' I explained who I was.

'Steve!' Mrs Millace said. 'Steve's hurt!'

'It's not bad,' I said quickly. 'It's just his collar bone.'

I went outside and told Steve. 'Why?' he asked tiredly as he walked slowly to the front door. 'What for?'

The policeman was asking the same question. 'Mrs Millace, please try to answer. What did they want?'

'They wanted the safe. I told them we didn't have one.' Mrs Millace began to cry and the tears joined the blood on her face. 'One of the men hit me. The other one broke the furniture.'

'I'll kill them!' Steve said angrily. 'We don't have a safe.'

'Can you remember anything about their car?'

Mrs Millace shook her head. 'It was dark. Anyway, I don't notice cars much.'

Then the doctor arrived.

'Don't go yet,' Steve said to me. There was a desperate expression on his face, and in the end I stayed all night. Mrs Millace went to hospital and then I cooked some supper. After that, I began to make the sitting room tidy. I put away a lot of magazines and newspapers and then picked up a small orange box.

'Where shall I put this?' I asked Steve.

'That's Dad's box of photographic rubbish,' he said. 'He never threw it away. He usually kept it in the fridge.'

I picked up a large black envelope which contained a piece of clear thick plastic. There was a piece of film, some negatives, and another very dark photograph in an envelope.

'Those were all in Dad's box of rubbish,' Steve said. 'He wanted to remember his worst mistakes. You can throw them away.'

I put George's worst mistakes into his rubbish box. Why had George kept them? I wanted to discover why.

'I hate those men,' Steve said. 'Why did they do this?'

I looked at Steve. He was exhausted and there were tears in his eyes.

'Come on,' I said. 'Time for bed.'

I woke up early the next morning, but I didn't want to get up. I wanted to avoid my problems. Other people had always decided my life for me. I had only lived with my

11

mother from time to time. She had left me with many different friends. I learned photography because she left me with Charlie. I became a jockey because she left me with a trainer. Now, I didn't want to become involved with Steve's problems. I didn't want to lose my job with Harold.

I got up and looked at George Millace's darkroom. The shelves were empty. The burglars had taken everything – his machines, his boxes of negatives and photographs, his films.

I left soon afterwards. I took with me George's box of rubbish.

'Can I take it?' I asked Steve.

'Of course,' Steve said. 'I know that you like photography. Dad liked that old rubbish, too, so you take it.'

He watched me put the box in the car, with my two camera bags.

'You never go anywhere without a camera, do you?' he said. 'You're just like Dad.'

I drove home then, for my Sunday meeting with Harold.

■ ■ ■ ■ ■
3
■ ■ ■ ■ ■

No more cheating

Sundays at six o'clock I always walked up the road to see
Harold Osborne. We had a drink, talked about the past
week, and discussed plans for the week ahead.

This Sunday, Harold had a visitor. I walked through
his house from the stable entrance and went into the
comfortable sitting room. And there, in one of the
armchairs, was Victor Briggs.

'Philip!' Harold said, with a smile. 'Get yourself a
drink. We're just going to watch the video of the race
yesterday. Sit down. Are you ready?'

Victor was wearing a dark suit. He didn't smile, but he
shook my hand.

The video began. We watched Daylight jumping
strongly and smoothly over the first fences. Then round
the bend and faster down the hill. Everything looked all
right. Then the fall, the rider over the horse's neck and
down under his feet. Silently, we watched the rest of the
race.

Harold stood up and turned off the video. He was six
feet tall, with red hair. He was fifty-two and looked ten
years younger. He smiled. 'I've watched it twenty times.
It's impossible to guess the truth.'

'Nobody suspected,' Victor said. 'Everyone said that it

was bad luck.' He picked up an envelope and held it out to me. 'This is my thank you, Philip.'

'It's very kind of you, Mr Briggs. But nothing's changed. I don't like you paying me when I lose like that.'

Victor Briggs said nothing. He put the envelope down again.

Harold was angry. 'Philip!' he said loudly. 'Don't be so stupid. There's a lot of money in that envelope. Victor's being very generous. Take it, and thank him, and shut up.'

'I'd – rather not.'

'I don't care if you'd rather not. You lost the race, didn't you? You'll take that money!'

'No, I won't. And,' I went on slowly, 'I don't want to do it any longer.'

'You'll lose if you're told to lose,' Harold said.

Victor stood up then, and they both looked down at me. I stood up, too.

'Please . . . don't ask me to lose again,' I said, as calmly as I could.

Victor was still silent.

'Look,' I said. 'If a horse is ill, of course I'll give him an easy ride. But no more like Daylight yesterday.'

Harold said coldly, 'You'd better go now, Philip. I'll talk to you in the morning.'

And so I left. I walked in the windy darkness down the road from Harold's house to mine, perhaps for the last time. Three years ago I had lost races for Harold and

Victor picked up an envelope and held it out to me.

Victor; but I knew that I could not cheat again. When had I changed? I didn't know. I only knew that I couldn't turn back.

I picked up George Millace's box of rubbish from the car and opened it on the table in the kitchen. Why had George kept this rubbish? His mistakes didn't look interesting or special. I was disappointed.

Just then, Jeremy Folk arrived. Jeremy was about twenty-five, very tall and very thin. He was a lawyer and a good friend of mine.

'Well, I say, I'm awfully sorry . . .' he said.

I smiled. 'Come in. It's all right. I'm not busy. Coffee?'

We went through into the kitchen and I made coffee. Jeremy looked at George Millace's box of rubbish.

'It's just rubbish,' I said. I picked up the envelope and slid out the dark photograph on to my hand . . . and found George's pot of gold.

It was not, at first sight, very exciting.

On the back of the photograph was another envelope and in that envelope was the negative. The photograph was black and grey, but the negative itself was clear and sharp.

'What is it?' Jeremy asked. 'Is it important?'

I shook my head. 'I don't know. Let's find out.'

I went into my darkroom, which was next to the kitchen. Jeremy followed. I turned off the white light and made four prints. They were clear, but none of them looked exactly like George's print. I started again. This time, I left the photograph in the developer too long. I lifted the paper out. What I had then was another print exactly like George's.

'The photographer left the print in the developer too long,' I explained. 'It's an easy mistake. But why keep it, with the negative? Why not throw it away?'

I turned on the white light and looked at my first four clear prints. Immediately, I understood why George had kept the negative.

It was a picture of two men who were sitting together in the sun outside a French café. There were coffee cups on the table and the men were talking to each other. Two men who said that they had never met.

One of the men was Elgin Yaxley. Two years ago he had owned five expensive horses. One day, out in the fields, they were all shot dead. Terence O'Tree, the man on the right in the photograph, had shot them. All five horses were insured and Elgin Yaxley had received a lot of money from the insurers. Terence O'Tree had gone to prison for two years. Elgin Yaxley had collected his money and then disappeared to Hong Kong.

'Yaxley told the police that he had never met O'Tree,' I told Jeremy. 'The police found no proof. But George did. Look at the date on that newspaper in the photograph – nearly two years ago.'

George had seen Yaxley and O'Tree in France and had

taken a photograph. He hadn't gone to the police. He had hidden the negative.

And now he was dead, and burglars were very interested in his house . . .

■ ■ ■ ■ ■
4
■ ■ ■ ■ ■

Ivor den Relgan

On Monday, Harold told me that I must choose.

'I don't want to lose you, Philip,' he said, 'but I need Victor. You've been racing for ten years. You won't go on for ever. Three or four more years. I need Victor's horses. I need his money.'

I stared at Harold.

'Let me know,' he said.

'All right.'

'I want you to stay.'

I was surprised, but also pleased. 'Thanks,' I said.

Nothing happened on Tuesday. On Wednesday at Kempton races I learnt that Ivor den Relgan had joined the Jockey Club; and Steve Millace's house had burned down.

'Ivor den Relgan!' All the jockeys were talking about it. 'Extraordinary!'

Ivor den Relgan was a very rich man, but very unpopular. The Jockey Club was a group of men, usually famous or successful, who were the law-makers and judges of the horse-racing world. They were mostly rich men, but rich men who were serious and responsible. Ivor den Relgan was neither. For a long time den Relgan had wanted to join the Jockey Club but the Club had always refused. And now suddenly they had changed their minds.

Steve Millace was waiting for me in the weighing room. 'Have you heard?' His face was white and his expression was desperate.

'Yes.'

'It happened yesterday. The whole place has gone.'

'Your mother wasn't there?'

'She's still in hospital. It's too much for her.' He was trembling. 'What shall I do? Tell me.'

I began to change my clothes.

'Please! Please help me!'

'All right,' I said at last. 'Do you want me to visit your mother in hospital?'

'Yes. Oh, thank you. Will you phone me?'

I went out to ride. The horse ran well, and we won. My second horse won, too, and I was full of happiness. I couldn't possibly stop racing, I told myself.

Mrs Millace lay alone in hospital. Her face was covered with bruises: red, grey, black and yellow.

'Steve asked me to come,' I said. 'He can't drive, because of his collar bone. I'm so sorry about the house.'

Mrs Millace opened one eye. 'George said that you took photographs, like he did.'

'Not like he did,' I said. 'George was the best.'

Mrs Millace tried to smile.

'About George's photographs,' I began.

Her smile disappeared. 'The police came today,' she said. 'They said that the fire wasn't an accident. They asked me whether George had any enemies.' She moved her head unhappily.

'Did George have any photographs which were worth burning?' I asked gently.

'George wouldn't . . .' she said.

George had, I thought. 'I'm terribly sorry,' I said. 'I agree with the police. George had something which someone desperately wanted to destroy. But don't worry. It has probably gone with the house.'

Mrs Millace began to tremble. 'George didn't . . . I know George . . . George didn't blackmail anyone.'

'Don't worry. It's all over now.'

I went home and looked again at the photograph of Elgin Yaxley and Terence O'Tree. Nobody knew that I had the negative. Nobody would burn my house or beat me. I left George's box of rubbish on the table in the kitchen.

The next day I rode again for Victor Briggs. Ivor den Relgan was standing outside the weighing room. He was tall and good-looking, with thick grey hair. He was wearing an expensive soft brown coat.

'Ride to win,' Harold said. 'There's a special silver cup for the winner of this race.'

And I did win. Harold was delighted and Victor smiled. We went to receive the cup which was given by

'Well done Mr Nore,' Dana said to me, and gave me the cup.

Miss Dana den Relgan. Ivor den Relgan's daughter was a small, extremely pretty girl with long fair hair and beautiful eyes.

'Well done, Mr Nore!' she said to me, and gave me the cup.

Lord White was standing next to her. He smiled and touched her hand. Lord White was the leader of the Jockey Club. He was about fifty-five, with white hair and bright blue eyes. He was a popular person, and so was his wife. I saw immediately that Lord White was very fond – too fond – of Dana den Relgan. Had the Jockey Club allowed Ivor den Relgan to join because Lord White had fallen in love with Dana? Everyone would think so.

As I showed Victor and Harold the silver cup, a small man, aged about thirty-five, with dark hair and glasses, walked up to Dana den Relgan and began speaking softly into her ear. She turned and began to walk slowly away with him.

As soon as Ivor den Relgan saw them, he stopped smiling and ran after his daughter. He took the man by the shoulder and threw him violently to the ground.

'Don't come near her!' den Relgan said.

'Who is that man?' I asked Victor Briggs quietly.

'Lance Kinship. He makes films,' Victor replied.

'And why the trouble?'

Victor knew the answer. 'Drugs,' he said finally. 'He goes to parties and gives stupid little girls dangerous white powder. Very fashionable.'

Very fashionable. But I didn't like it because my mother had taken drugs.

We watched as Lance Kinship picked himself up. 'If I want to talk to Dana, I'll talk to her,' he said.

'Not while I'm here, you won't,' said den Relgan.

Lance Kinship seemed unafraid. 'Little girls don't always have their daddies with them,' he said angrily; and den Relgan hit him, hard and sharp, on the nose.

Noses bleed easily and there was a lot of blood. It ran down Kinship's mouth and chin and dropped on to his coat.

Lord White looked uncomfortable. 'Emergency room, don't you think?' He looked round, and saw me. 'Er . . . Nore, take this man to the emergency room, will you, please? Awfully good of you.'

Kinship followed me to the emergency room. As we passed, den Relgan spoke.

'If you come near Dana again, I'll break your neck.'

■ ■ ■ ■ ■
5
■ ■ ■ ■ ■
Another secret

Perhaps Elgin Yaxley had burnt George Millace's house, I thought. I asked the man who had trained Yaxley's horses about him.

'He's in Hong Kong. He lives there now. Why?'

'I just thought . . . that I saw him last week.'

'Well, you're wrong,' the trainer said. 'I had a letter yesterday from Elgin, from Hong Kong, posted on the day of George Millace's funeral.'

'He was sorry about George's death, was he?'

The trainer laughed. 'Are you crazy? You knew George.'

Elgin Yaxley was in Hong Kong. Terence O'Tree was still in prison. I was wrong, then. Someone else had burned George Millace's house.

I tried to forget the mystery of George Millace, and turned my mind to the races. I was at Windsor and I was going to ride an old horse in his last race. Several horses fell during the race, and my horse won.

He was exhausted, but his owner – a dear old lady – was delighted.

'I knew that he'd do it one day,' she said enthusiastically. 'I knew that he would. Isn't he a grand old boy!'

'Grand,' I agreed.

'This is his last season, you know. His last race.' She spoke to the horse. 'We're all getting older, aren't we, old boy? We can't go on for ever. Everything ends, doesn't it, old boy? But today it's been grand.'

I went into the weighing room and her words came with me: everything ends, but today it's been grand. Ten years had been grand, but everything ends.

Life changes, everything ends. I didn't want to stop racing. I didn't want Victor Briggs to stop me. But I myself was changing.

Outside the weighing room, I was suddenly popular. I had won four races in one week, and five trainers offered me horses for next week. I accepted, and pushed these uncomfortable ideas out of my head.

Jeremy Folk came to visit on Sunday, and followed me through into the kitchen.

'Champagne?' I asked. I picked a bottle out of the fridge.

'It's . . . er . . . only ten o'clock,' he said.

'Four winners, in one week,' I said. 'Would you rather have coffee?'

'Er . . . actually . . . no.'

We sat in the kitchen and drank champagne and looked at George Millace's box of rubbish.

'I want to spend today on that,' I said.

Jeremy opened the box and lifted the things out. He was disappointed. 'These are nothing – just rubbish.'

'Mmm.' I picked up a piece of clear-looking film. 'Look at that, against the light.'

He took the piece of film and held it up. 'I can see some shadows,' he said.

'They're pictures,' I said. 'I've already found one very interesting photograph in that box. Perhaps these pictures will be interesting, too.'

We went into the darkroom and I searched in one of the cupboards for the special chemical I needed. I turned off the white light and turned on the red light. I began to print the negative with the special chemical.

Jeremy watched. 'Can't see anything,' he said.

I agreed. I tried four times, but only shadows appeared.

We went back into the kitchen and drank some more champagne.

'I think I'll print that negative on to another film, not on to paper,' I said.

'Can you do that?'

'Oh yes. You can print on to anything, if you want to. Black and white, of course, not colour.'

'You love doing this, don't you?'

I drank some more champagne. 'I suppose I do,' I agreed.

This time, I printed the negatives on to a new film. Then, I developed those prints into new negatives.

'Why are you smiling?' Jeremy asked.

'Take a look,' I said.

He held the negatives up to the light. 'I can't see anything.'

'They're three pictures of a man and a girl. Let's print black and white pictures from the new negatives.'

I tried several times before I got three good prints. I put on the white light and looked at them carefully.

The pictures were now very clear. A man holding and kissing a girl. Neither of them was wearing any clothes, and there could be no doubt that they were lovers.

'That's extraordinary! Well done!' said Jeremy. He laughed. 'But they're not photos that you'd print in a newspaper, are they?'

I was silent, and Jeremy looked at me closely.

'What is it? What's the matter?'

'They're disastrous,' I said at last. 'I know those two people. I think that George Millace was blackmailing people.'

We went back into the kitchen. 'Look at that box of rubbish,' I said. 'I've discovered two of George's secrets. Perhaps that box is full of secrets.'

'Are you . . . er . . . going to tell me about all this?' Jeremy asked.

So I told him about George Millace. I told him about the burglars, about Mrs Millace, about the fire. I told him about Elgin Yaxley and Terence O'Tree and the five horses. And I told him about the man and the girl.

Jeremy shook his head. 'Destroy everything,' he said.

'Well, no,' I said slowly. 'I want to discover George's secrets. I want to discover who burnt George's house.'

Jeremy stood up and walked restlessly around the

I tried several times before I got three good prints.

room. 'I don't like it,' he said. 'It's dangerous.'

'Nobody knows that I've got George's things.'

'Well . . . was there any doubt . . . about George's death?'

I felt suddenly sick. 'Oh no!' I said.

'What happened exactly?'

'He was driving home from Doncaster and he went to sleep and ran into a tree.'

'Is that all?'

I thought. 'Well, his son Steve said that George stopped at a friend's house for a drink. Then he drove on towards home and hit the tree.'

Jeremy turned to me. 'Give it up,' he said. 'Burn those pictures.'

'I'm surprised!' I said. 'You're a lawyer. Those photographs are important.'

'Stop laughing!' he said. 'You may drive into a tree, too!'

■ ■ ■ ■ ■

6

■ ■ ■ ■ ■

Search for Samantha

Jeremy left at six o'clock and I walked up the road to meet Harold. He had six horses for me during the week, and with the five extra horses I had been given, I was going to have a busy week.

'Next Saturday at Ascot, two of Victor's horses are running,' he said. 'Chainmail . . . and Daylight.'

I looked at him quickly. 'I'm not going to cheat,' I said.

'Philip . . .'

'You tell me, Harold,' I said. 'Tell me early on Saturday morning, and I'll be ill. Sick.'

'But . . .'

I controlled my anger. 'We had four winners last week,' I said. 'Isn't that enough for you?'

'But if Victor . . .'

I said, 'I'll ride as hard as I can for Victor – even if it breaks my neck. You know that. But I'll ride to win. You tell Victor that.' I stood up. I was unable to sit calmly. 'And don't forget, Harold, that Daylight is only four. He's fast and strong and brave and I like him; and I'm not going to destroy his enthusiasm. And you *will* destroy it, if you carry on. It's stupid, as well as dishonest.'

'Have you finished?'

'Yes.'

31

'I agree with you and I'll tell Victor. But in the end, it's Victor's horse.'

I was silent.

'If it's necessary,' Harold said unhappily, 'I'll tell you early on Saturday, so that you can be sick.'

On Monday I rode three horses. One came second, one came third, and one fell at the last fence. On Tuesday I was not riding, and I felt too restless to work in my dark-room. I was worried about Victor Briggs and what was going to happen next Saturday. If Victor said he didn't want me to ride his horses again . . . Were my racing days coming to an end? What job could I do next? I only knew how to ride race-horses. I felt that I was at a crossroads in my life – a very lonely crossroads.

My mother was dead, and I'd never known who my father was. Perhaps he was dead too. I couldn't remember my mother very clearly. Charlie, who had taught me about photography, I remembered very well. He had been like a father to me, but he was dead now. I could remember another of the friends that my mother had left me with several times – Samantha. She had been a warm-hearted, motherly woman – very kind to her small uninvited visitor. I suddenly felt a need to see Samantha again, not for advice, but just to make contact. I wanted to remind myself who I was, where I had come from. Perhaps then I would know where I was going next.

I didn't know her last name or the exact address, but I

drove to Chiswick in London and began walking. All the houses looked the same. I found an old pub which I remembered, and I began knocking on the doors of houses in that street.

'Excuse me,' I said. 'Does Samantha live here?'

'Who?'

'Samantha.'

'No!' And the door shut.

I tried several houses, but the usual reply was a cold stare and then the door banged shut. It was no good, I thought. It was more than twenty years ago. Samantha had probably moved. I tried another house where no one answered, and another where a grey-haired woman opened the door. I looked at her.

'What do you want?' she asked.

'Are you . . .' I began slowly, 'Samantha?'

'What do you want?' she asked again.

'Do you remember the name Nore? I'm . . . Philip Nore. My mother was Caroline Nore.'

The woman was surprised, then smiled. 'You'd better come in,' she said. 'I'm Samantha Bergen.'

I went up the steps and followed the woman into the kitchen. There was a big table and chairs, and a big window which opened on to the garden. A pretty girl of about twenty, with short dark hair and large grey eyes, was sitting at the table.

'This is my daughter, Clare,' Samantha said. 'She wasn't born when you stayed here.' And to her daughter she said, 'This is Philip Nore. He stayed here now and then . . . more than twenty years ago!' She looked at me carefully. 'Yes, I can see now that you're Philip. How extraordinary to see you again!'

'Tell me about my mother,' I said. 'What was she like?'

'Caroline? So pretty. Full of light and fun. But . . .' she stopped.

'But what?' I asked. 'She died twelve years ago. I want to know the truth.'

'Well . . . she took drugs. Anything – everything. She tried them all. She brought you here about six times and left you here for months.'

'I wanted to find you – to say thank you,' I said. 'I've always been grateful to you.'

'Have you?' Samantha seemed pleased.

They gave me tea and were very friendly to me. We sat and talked and I told them that I was a jockey and lived in Lambourn.

'Aren't there lots of racing stables there?' Clare asked.

'That's right.'

'Hmm.' She thought for a minute. 'I'm going to ring up my boss. I work for a publisher, you see. We're doing a book on British villages, and we need another village. Would you mind?'

'Of course not.'

Clare went across to the telephone. Samantha looked at me. 'She's very enthusiastic,' she explained. 'I'm writing a cookery book for her.'

'I can see now that you're Philip. How extraordinary
to see you again!'

Clare finished talking on the telephone and came back to the table. 'He's interested. We'll go down and look at the village, and then the writer and photographer will go.'

'I've taken pictures of Lambourn . . . If you'd like to . . .'

She shook her head. 'We need professional photographs. Sorry. But we'll come and see you. Is that all right?'

'Yes.'

She gave me a sudden smile. 'Can we come on Friday?' she asked.

7

Jockey's life

Lance Kinship was making a film at Newbury on Wednesday. I picked up my Nikon and took a few pictures of the camera-men. Lance Kinship turned his head and saw me.

He looked annoyed, and marched across to me. 'What are you doing?'

'I'm just interested,' I said quietly.

He looked at my riding boots and my red and yellow shirt. 'A jockey,' he said to himself. 'With a Nikon.'

'How's the nose?' I asked politely.

He didn't answer. 'Don't get into my film,' he said. 'I don't want a jockey with a Nikon in my film.'

'I'll be careful,' I said. And I took some more pictures of Lance Kinship as he gave orders to the men with their big cameras.

I had only one race that day, and I fell off at the eighth fence, where the horse put his feet wrong and fell over the fence. I went back to the weighing room.

Lance Kinship was waiting for me. 'Oh, there you are,' he said. 'What's your name?'

'Philip Nore.'

'Well, Phil. You took some photographs today, right? Are they good ones? I'll buy the good ones. How's that?'

'Well . . .' I was surprised. 'Yes, if you like.'

'Good. I had a photographer who was going to take some pictures of me while I was making this film. But he died. I asked the news photographers, but they're all busy. Then I thought of you, right?'

I asked him which photographer had died.

'Man called Millace. Know him?'

'I knew him,' I said.

Lance Kinship gave me a card with his address on it. It was my first job as a professional photographer!

When I reached home I turned on the lights and pulled the curtains across the windows. I sat down at the table in the kitchen and looked again at the rubbish in George Millace's box. I wanted to discover his secrets. But what would I do with the secrets? I didn't know.

I lifted out the large black envelope from the bottom of the box. Inside there was a piece of paper and a piece of clear plastic. Why had George kept them in a black envelope? I put them back. Then I looked at the colour negatives in the box. There were thirty-six negatives. Some of them were orange and some of them were orange with red shapes on them. Perhaps yellow pictures were hidden under the orange negatives.

I went into the darkroom and turned on the colour developer. I discovered almost at once that under the orange there was yellow, which became blue when I printed it. But not pictures in blue. Just squares of blue.

I ended with thirty-six blue prints, some with green shapes on them.

I washed the prints and dried them. Then I looked at them carefully. There were darker shapes on some of them. When I realized the truth, I was too tired to start again. I cleaned the darkroom and went to bed.

I telephoned Jeremy Folk the next morning. 'I've been working,' I said. 'And printing.'

'From that box?' he asked.

'Yes.'

'Don't do it,' he said. And then, 'What have you found?'

'Blue prints. Deep blue. George Millace put a blue filter on to his camera and photographed a black and white picture on to a colour negative film.'

'I don't understand.'

'I'm talking about Millace. Clever, dangerous Millace. As soon as I print those pictures, another Millace secret will be in our hands.'

'I seriously think that you should burn it all.'

'Not a chance.'

'You think it's a game. It's not a game. Be careful.'

I said that I would be careful. It was easy to say.

Early on Friday morning Clare Bergen appeared at my front door with a young man who was her boss. I drove them through the village and up on to the hills so that they could see the horses.

'I'll walk round the village myself,' said the young man.

Clare and I went back to my house for coffee. Clare looked at the darkroom.

'You said that you took photographs,' she said slowly.

'Yes, I do. It's my hobby.'

'But I thought that you meant . . .' She looked at me. 'I had no idea . . .'

'It doesn't matter,' I said.

'Well . . . can I see them?'

We went into the sitting room with our coffee. I pulled open a cupboard and took out some boxes. 'Here you are – Lambourn village.'

'What are those others?'

'Just pictures.'

She looked at the boxes and read aloud. 'America. Lambourn. Children. France. Harold's stables. Jockey's Life . . . What's Jockey's Life? Can I look?'

'Of course.'

Clare opened the box and began to look at the photographs. Silently.

'Can I see Lambourn?' she said at last.

I gave her the Lambourn box and she looked at those. Silently.

'I know they're not wonderful,' I said quietly. 'You don't need to say something kind.'

She looked up at me sharply. 'You know perfectly well that they're good.' She closed the boxes and stared down at them. 'I've been looking for something like you.'

'Something?'

Clare opened the box and began to look at the photographs.

'Yes. I need . . . I want . . . a successful book. I've been looking for that book for two years now – looking and not finding, because I want something special. And now I've found it.'

I was surprised. 'But Lambourn isn't special!' I said.

Clare put her hand on the Jockey's Life box. 'Not Lambourn,' she said. 'This. Have any of these photographs appeared in newspapers or magazines?'

I shook my head. 'I've never tried.'

'You're extraordinary. Your photographs are fantastic and you don't know it. A jockey's life is all there – the hard work, the bad weather, the happiness, the pain. I know it all. I see everything, because of your pictures. Promise me something? Don't sell those pictures to someone else.'

'All right.'

'And don't tell my boss when he comes back. I want this to be my book, not his.'

I smiled. 'All right.'

I put the box back into the cupboard. When her boss returned, he saw only the photographs of Lambourn. He liked them and agreed to buy some, and soon afterwards he and Clare left.

I was pleased because they liked my work. Work? The word filled me with alarm. I had never called my photographs work before. No, I thought, I'm a jockey!

8

Ride to win

On Saturday Harold phoned at a quarter to ten.

'Victor rang just now,' he said. 'I told him that Daylight must be ridden carefully. I told him that you should ride to win.'

'What happened?'

'He said yes!' Harold shouted. 'He's changed his mind! You can win on his horses. And you'd better make sure that you do win!'

I went to Ascot. Outside the weighing room stood Ivor den Relgan. He was smiling. Lord White was there, too. He was holding the lovely Dana's arm. Behind them stood Lady White, thin and unhappy.

'Ivor den Relgan is making trouble in the Jockey Club. He must be stopped,' Harold said angrily.

My first race was on Daylight. I rode hard and dangerously, and Daylight raced well. We tried our best, but another horse passed us at the last fence and we didn't win.

'Sorry,' I said to Harold.

Harold said nothing. Victor Briggs was silent, his face without expression.

I went out again to ride Chainmail. 'Don't kill yourself,' Harold said.

Chainmail was a young, strong horse who wanted to win. He needed to be controlled by a calm rider, but that day I rode like a madman. However, another horse ran better. In fact, two horses ran better and Chainmail came third.

Again, Victor Briggs stared at me without a word. He wanted winners and I gave him two losers. I felt terribly tired.

On my way to the car park I met Mrs Millace. She looked much better.

'Can I talk to you?' she asked.

'Of course,' I said. 'Let's have some coffee.'

We went into a café and sat down. 'I've been talking to Lady White,' Mrs Millace said. 'She's an old friend of mine. She's desperate about Dana den Relgan.'

'Do you know the den Relgans?'

'No, I don't, although George saw them in St Tropez last summer.' She paused. 'But I didn't want to talk about this. I wanted to thank you for your help.'

'I was happy to help,' I said. 'In fact, I want to ask you something. Do you know where George stopped for a drink, on his way home from Doncaster?'

'Of course I know. He saw a man called Lance Kinship, who makes films. He wanted George to take some pictures of him.'

I told her that I had taken the pictures of Lance Kinship.

Mrs Millace smiled. 'George always said that you

would take his job one day. I wish he knew. I wish . . . oh, dear!'

Mrs Millace began to cry. 'I'm sorry,' she said.

'It's natural to cry,' I said gently. It was only three weeks since George had died.

'I remember the very last thing which he said to me,' she said. 'He asked me to buy some ammonia. It's stupid, isn't it? I don't even know . . . I don't even know what he wanted it for.'

Later, I saw Lance Kinship and gave him the pictures of himself as a film-maker. He took them out of the envelope and looked at them.

'Well, well,' he said. 'I like them.' He pulled out his wallet and paid me in cash. 'Make me two more copies of all of them. Right?'

At that moment Jeremy appeared. I introduced him to Lance.

'George Millace had a drink at Lance's house before his accident,' I added.

Kinship looked at us sharply. 'A great photographer, George,' he said. 'Very sad.' He looked through my photographs again. 'Very nice photographs, these. Want to see?' He passed them to Jeremy.

Jeremy looked at them carefully. 'You must be an important man,' he said.

Kinship smiled happily. 'Two more copies of them all,' he said again, and walked away.

Lance Kinship smiled happily. 'Two more copies of them all,'
he said.

At that moment I saw something extraordinary. I stood and stared. 'Do you see', I said to Jeremy, 'that man over there?'

'Yes.'

'He's one of the men in that photograph of the French café. That's Elgin Yaxley.'

Three weeks after George's death, two weeks after the fire; and Elgin Yaxley was home from Hong Kong!

Jeremy said, 'That's extraordinary. He looks terribly pleased with himself. You've still got that photograph?'

'I surely have.'

We stood and watched Elgin Yaxley as he talked to a trainer.

'What will you do with it?'

'Just wait, I suppose,' I said. 'Tomorrow I'm going to work on the blue prints.'

'You think you can do it?'

'I hope so. With luck.'

George's letters

I went into my darkroom on Sunday morning and prepared the developer. I was going to print George's colour negatives on to black and white paper. I put the thirty-six negatives into the machine and put the blue filter on to the machine.

I stood in the red light and watched. I tried several times, but nothing happened. At last I saw that six of the negatives had grey shapes on them. I began to smile. I had almost discovered another of George's photographic secrets.

My hands trembled as I enlarged one print, washed it, and carried it into the kitchen. The print was still wet, but I could read it without difficulty. It was a letter. Written by George Millace.

Dear Elgin Yaxley
You will be interested in this photograph. You told the police that you had never met this man.
The Jockey Club would be interested in this photograph. And the police.
I will ring you soon, however, with another idea.
Yours sincerely
George Millace

I read the letter again. If I enlarged and read the other letters on the other negatives, I would learn all George's secrets. What would I do with them?

I went upstairs into the sitting room and looked out of the window for a while. I thought of Elgin Yaxley yesterday, happy and confident. I thought of the five horses. Terence O'Tree in prison. All the money.

I couldn't decide what to do.

After a while I went back to the darkroom. I printed the five other negatives. They were five more letters. Two of them were also to Elgin Yaxley. One was to a trainer about two horses both called Amber Globe. Another letter was about the lovers. 'The Jockey Club would be interested in this photograph,' the letters ended. 'I will ring you soon, however, with another idea.'

The fifth letter made me laugh and took away my fear.

I went back into the kitchen and rang Lord White.

'You want to see me? What about?' he asked.

'About George Millace, sir.'

'Photographer? Died recently?'

'Yes, sir. Mrs Millace is a friend of Lady White.'

'Yes, yes,' he said impatiently. 'I could see you at Kempton, if you like.'

'I would like to see you at home.'

'Very well, very well. Five o'clock on Tuesday.'

After that, I drove to London to see Clare.

'Come in and have a drink,' Clare said. She was wearing a red shirt and black trousers and looked very pretty. 'I watched you on television on Saturday,' she said. 'It's terribly dangerous, isn't it?'

'Not always like Saturday,' I answered.

'What happens if you're badly injured?'

'You mend as fast as possible and get back to work.'

'And what if it's too bad to mend?'

'You've got a problem. But there's always the Injured Jockeys Fund.'

'What's that?'

'It helps the wives and children of dead and injured jockeys.'

'I suppose that's better than nothing,' Clare said.

We went out a little later and ate dinner in a small French restaurant. We talked about my photographs and I told her about those I had taken of Lance Kinship.

'Your work is good,' Clare said. 'You need someone who can sell your pictures for you. How about me?'

I was surprised. 'Yes, but . . .'

'No buts,' she said. 'Why take fantastic pictures if no one ever sees them?'

'But there are thousands of photographers.'

'There's always room for one more.' The light shone on her face and her grey eyes looked calmly into mine. 'I'd like to try. Will you let me try?'

Hope for the best, I thought. 'All right,' I said. And when we got back to her door, I kissed her. She seemed to like it.

10

Visit to Lord White

Four times on Tuesday morning I lifted the telephone in order to call Lord White. Four times I put the telephone down before his phone began to ring. Four times I decided that I must see Lord White.

I went. Lord White's house was in the country. A big, old house, with lots of trees. Lord White was in a small sitting room. He shook my hand and waited.

I sat down. 'Sir . . .' I began. 'I'm sorry, very sorry, sir . . . I'm afraid I have some rather painful news.'

Lord White shook his head. 'About George Millace? I don't understand.'

'Yes. About some photographs he took.' I stopped. It was difficult. I was going to hurt Lord White and I didn't want to do it.

'Go on, Nore,' Lord White said comfortably.

I opened the large envelope I carried and pulled out the three photographs of the lovers. I put one of the photographs into Lord White's hand. His love for Dana den Relgan was stupid, I thought, but I felt deeply sorry for him.

He looked at the photograph. At first he was extremely angry. 'Why are you doing this?' he asked. The photograph shook in his hand. 'This is terrible!'

I put one of the photographs into Lord White's hand.

I put the other two photos on the table. 'As you will see,' I said quietly, 'the others are worse.'

Slowly, Lord White picked up the photographs. He looked at them silently. His face showed his horror and anger.

The man who was holding Dana in his arms was Ivor den Relgan.

'They say,' Lord White said, 'that cameras do lie.' His voice trembled.

'Not this one.'

'It can't be true.'

I took from the envelope a print of the letter which George Millace had written to Ivor den Relgan, and gave it to Lord White.

Dear Ivor den Relgan

You will be interested in these photographs which I took a few days ago in St Tropez. The photographs show you with a young lady. You say that this young lady is your daughter. Why are you pretending?

Are you hoping to join the Jockey Club – by trapping an important person?

I could send these photographs to Lord White. I will ring you soon, however, with another idea.

Yours sincerely
George Millace

Lord White grew older as he read the letter. His face

became grey. I looked at my hands, my feet, out of the window.

After a very long time he said, 'Where did you get these photographs?'

'George Millace's son gave me a box of things, after George died. These photos were in it.'

He was silent again. Then he said, 'Why did you bring them to me?'

I said quietly, 'Perhaps you haven't noticed, but people have become worried recently about Ivor den Relgan.'

Lord White stared at me with his blue eyes. 'And you are trying to stop that?'

'Sir . . . yes.'

He looked angry. 'It's not your business, Nore.'

I didn't answer at once. He was right: it wasn't my business. But . . . In the end I said, 'Sir, why was Ivor den Relgan at last allowed to join the Jockey Club? Because you were fond of Dana den Relgan? If you truly believe that Ivor den Relgan is a suitable person for the Jockey Club, then I apologize.'

'Please leave,' Lord White said angrily.

I stood up and walked over to the door. But when I reached it, I heard his voice from behind me.

'Wait, Nore. I must think. Will you please come back and sit down?'

I returned to the armchair. He went and stood by the window and looked at the garden.

'How many people have seen these pictures?'

'Only one friend. Not a racing person.'

'Did you discuss this with anyone before you came here?'

'No, sir.'

'Are you going to talk about this at the races?'

'No!' I was angry. 'I am not.'

'And do you . . .' He stopped, but then went on, 'Do you expect any . . . money?'

I stood up immediately. I was hurt and angry. 'I do not,' I said. 'I'm not George Millace. I think . . . I think that I'll go now.'

And I went, out of the room, out of his house.

11

The other idea

Newbury races, Friday, late November.

Lord White was there. He was standing under the glass roof outside the weighing room. He looked the same: white hair, brown coat, dark grey suit. I passed near him but he continued to talk to two other members of the Jockey Club. If he didn't want to talk to me, I didn't mind. Less difficult.

I went out for my first ride. As Harold helped me up, he smiled widely. 'Did you hear that den Relgan is out of the Jockey Club?'

I looked at him sharply. 'Are you sure?'

'I'm sure,' Harold said. 'They had an emergency meeting of the Jockey Club in London this morning. He's out.'

'Everyone will be pleased,' I said as I got up on the horse.

I had two races. I finished second, and then fourth. A normal day.

On Saturday I rode Sharpener, who was one of Victor's horses.

'Ride Sharpener to win,' Harold said. 'But don't ride like a madman again.'

Outside the weighing room I saw Elgin Yaxley. What was I going to do about Elgin Yaxley?

Sharpener was the favourite, and he ran well and jumped well. We came in first.

A winner for Victor. Harold was very pleased.

I went in and changed and thought about Elgin Yaxley. In the end I went to my car and picked up the picture of Yaxley. Then I went and found Yaxley.

'Can I talk to you for a moment?'

'You're not going to ride my new horses,' Yaxley said. 'So don't ask.'

'I don't want to ride your horses,' I said.

'What do you want then?'

'I want to give you a message,' I said. 'A private message. From George Millace.'

His face went white and his moustache began to tremble.

'I have a photograph which you ought to see,' I said.

I passed the envelope to him and he looked at the picture. Of Terence O'Tree with himself in the café. His hands were trembling and on his face was an expression of fear. His mouth opened, but no words came out.

'The police would like copies of that picture,' I said.

Yaxley still could not speak.

'There's another way,' I said. 'George's way.'

Yaxley hated me. I saw it in his eyes. But I wanted to find out what George had done.

'I want the same as George,' I said coldly.

'I want the same as George,' I said coldly.

'No!' His voice was full of horror; empty of hope. 'I haven't got it. Not ten.'

I stared at him, and said nothing.

'It hasn't been easy,' he begged. 'Can't you leave me alone? George said only once . . . and now *you*! Five, then. Is that all right? That's enough. I haven't got any more.'

I continued to stare, and waited.

'All right, then. Seven and a half.' He was shaking with anger and fear. 'That's all . . . You're worse than George Millace!'

He brought out his cheque book and a pen. He wrote a cheque. 'Not Hong Kong,' he said wildly. 'I don't like it there.'

I stared again. Suddenly, I understood. 'Oh . . . Anywhere. Anywhere out of Britain.' I took the cheque and he turned and walked away.

I was going to destroy the cheque. But when I looked at that cheque, a bright light exploded in my head – a light of excitement and understanding. I had used George's picture and his letter. I had used his cruelty, his 'other idea'.

Now I had it. All of it. Elgin Yaxley was going to leave Britain and I held his cheque for seven thousand five hundred pounds.

The cheque was made out not to me, but to the Injured Jockeys Fund.

Not careful enough

I walked around for a while and tried to find the ex-
jockey who managed the Injured Jockeys Fund. At last I
found him in the private bar of a television company.

He held up his glass. 'Want a drink?' he asked.

I shook my head. 'I'm riding in a minute. I just want to
give you a cheque.'

He stared at the cheque. 'Wonderful!' he said.

'Is it the first time that Yaxley's been so generous?'

'No, it isn't,' he said. 'He gave us ten thousand a few
months ago, just before he went to Hong Kong. We took
it, of course, but we wondered . . . He'd just been paid a
hundred thousand for those horses that were shot . . .'

'Well, he's going abroad again, and he gave me this
cheque for you,' I explained. 'Have you had any other
large cheques like that?'

'Not many as large as this, no. Ivor den Relgan gave us
a thousand at the beginning of the season. Very generous.'

He went back to the bar and I returned to the weighing
room. I was as bad as George, I thought. Just as bad. It
didn't seem so wrong, now that I had done it myself.

'Watch this horse,' Harold said. 'He made a lot of
mistakes during his last race. He needs a good view of
each fence.'

'OK,' I said.

I kept the horse in front. Over the first fence. Good jump, no trouble. Over the second . . . Over the third . . . Suddenly the horse's feet touched the top of the fence. He and I crashed to the grass together, and twenty-two horses came over the jump after us. It happened very fast.

It had happened before and it would happen again. I lay painfully on my side and looked at the grass. Nothing seemed to be broken. I got up slowly and went back to the weighing room in an ambulance. I saw the doctor, who said that no bones were broken. Harold was waiting.

'I'll drive you home,' he said. 'One of the boys can follow with your car.'

I agreed and we drove silently to Lambourn.

'A bad fall,' Harold said at last.

'Mmm. Is the horse all right?'

'Yes, stupid animal.'

'If Victor Briggs comes down here again,' I said, 'would you tell me?'

He looked sideways at me. 'You want to see him?'

'I want to know his plans.'

'Why not leave it?'

'I can't. Don't worry. I don't want to lose this job. I just want to talk to him.'

'All right,' Harold said doubtfully. He stopped his car beside my front door. 'Are you all right?' he asked. 'You're shaking.'

61

'I'll have a hot bath,' I replied. 'Thanks for the lift home.'

'You'll be better for next week? Tuesday at Plumpton?'

'Absolutely,' I said.

It was already dark. I turned on the lights and made some coffee. Bath, food, television, bed, I thought.

Mrs Jackson, my neighbour, came round. 'A man from the water company came to look round your house this morning,' she said. 'He wanted to check all the old pipes – he said there had been some problems. Anyway, he showed me his papers, and I came in with him.'

'That's fine, Mrs Jackson,' I said.

She went, and I telephoned Jeremy. I told him that I had news about Yaxley.

'I'll see you later,' he said.

'Not today,' I said. 'I'm going to bed early. Come tomorrow.'

I went to the bathroom and lay in the hot water for a long time. There were bruises all over my body.

At nine o'clock, the front door bell rang. I got dressed, and went and opened the door. Ivor den Relgan stood there. He was holding a gun.

'Move back,' he said. 'I'm coming in.'

I stepped backwards, afraid. I saw the hate in his eyes. He was certain to kill me. I felt light, empty.

He stepped through my door and kicked it shut behind him. 'George Millace was bad,' he said. 'You're worse.'

He was a man who loved to be important. I had shown

he was dishonest, a liar, a cheat. He had been thrown out of the Jockey Club because of me.

Be careful, Jeremy had said.

I hadn't been.

'Did you . . .' I said. My voice sounded strange. 'Did you burn his house?'

'Burnt! To the ground! And you had the photographs all the time!' he said angrily. 'Move back.' He waved the gun. 'Back there. Go on!'

I moved back past the darkroom door. I'll have to run, I thought wildly. I must try to escape.

Suddenly the kitchen door crashed open. Two men came into the hall fast, with masks over their faces.

I tried to fight them.

I tried, but I was bruised and torn already, because of my fall. I couldn't see, I couldn't shout. I could only just breathe. They hit my head, my face. When I fell on the ground, they used their boots. They kicked my arms, legs, back, stomach, head.

Everything went dark.

When I became conscious, it was quiet. I was lying on the floor. I'm alive, I thought. I tried to move. A bad mistake. My whole body screamed with pain. Perhaps I was going to die.

I lay quiet for hours. I waited to die, but I didn't. I lay on the floor all night and all morning. The blood on my face dried.

Somebody rang the front door bell.

When I fell on the ground, they used their boots.

I lifted my head and moved my arms, my legs. I tried to sit up, but I couldn't.

The bell rang again. Go away, I thought. I'm better alone.

Then I heard someone at the back door – the broken back door. It was Jeremy.

'Philip!' He knelt down beside me. 'Your face! You've got blood everywhere. Can you see? Your eyes are . . .' He stopped.

He wanted to move me, to wash me, to call a doctor. I wanted to stay quiet, until I could move myself.

'Well . . . do you want anything? Tea?'

'Find some champagne. Kitchen cupboard.'

Jeremy thought that I was mad, but he found a bottle and brought me a glass. I drank some of it.

The front door bell rang again. The visitor was Clare. She knelt beside me and said, 'This isn't a fall, is it? Someone's done this to you, haven't they?'

'Have some champagne.'

She stood up and fetched a glass.

'We must get a doctor,' said Jeremy.

'If he wants to lie on the floor, let him. He's been injured many times. He knows what's best.'

A girl who understands, I thought. Fantastic!

Clare and Jeremy sat in the kitchen and talked. I drank some more champagne and felt that soon I would sit up.

The front door bell rang again.

Clare walked to the front door. The girl outside pushed

past Clare. 'I must see,' she said desperately. 'I must know if he's alive.'

I knew her voice. I didn't need to see the desperate beautiful face which froze when it saw me. Dana den Relgan.

13

Dana is desperate

'Oh no!' she said.

'I *am* alive,' I said.

'He wasn't worried. He said that no one saw them, that it didn't matter if you died . . .'

Clare asked, 'You know who did this?'

Dana looked at her. 'I have to talk to him. Alone.'

'But he's . . .' Clare stopped, and said, 'Philip?'

'It's all right.'

'We'll be in the kitchen,' Clare said.

Dana sat down on the floor beside me. She was worried, afraid, desperate. 'Please,' she said. '*Please.*'

'Please . . . what?'

'Please give me . . . what I wrote for George Millace.'

I lay silent, my eyes shut.

'How can I ask you . . . when Ivor's done this to you? How can you be kind? Please, please, I beg you . . . give it back.'

'Is he your father?'

'No.' A whisper. 'It was Ivor's idea. He gives me money . . . I need money.'

'Does he know you're here?'

'No!' She was frightened. 'He hates drugs. I had to write that list for George Millace because he was going to show those pictures to Lord White. But you . . . you'll give it back to me, won't you? The list?'

'Where did you write the list?'

'On the packet of cigarettes, of course.' She stopped. 'You have got it, haven't you?'

'What did you write on the list?'

'You haven't got it!' She stood up. Her beautiful face was angry and ugly with fear. 'You haven't got it! I came here . . . I told you . . . all for nothing.' She turned and marched to the door. 'I wish that Ivor had killed you! I hope you *hurt*!'

Clare and Jeremy came out of the kitchen.

'What did she want?' Clare asked.

'Something that I haven't got. I'll tell you tomorrow.'

Clare sat beside me and put her hand on mine. 'Are you all right?'

'I want to get up,' I said. Slowly, I pulled myself on to my knees. Jeremy and Clare helped me to stand. The pain ran through my body, but I was up. Jeremy helped me to the bathroom.

'I'll wash the blood off the floor downstairs,' he said.

I looked at myself in the mirror. My face was red, blood everywhere. My mouth was cut, purple. Two broken teeth. A week, I thought. In a week I'd be better. I began to wash my face.

There was a heavy crash from downstairs. I pulled open the bathroom door and saw Clare coming from the kitchen.

'Are you all right?' she asked. 'Did you fall?'

'No. Must be Jeremy.'

We went through to the darkroom . . . and found Jeremy face down on the floor. A bowl of water had fallen beside him. There was a smell . . . a strong smell of bad eggs. A smell that I knew.

I caught Clare's arm and pulled her to the front door. Opened it. Pushed her outside.

'Stay there,' I said desperately. 'Stay outside. It's gas.'

I breathed the dark cold air deeply and turned back. I bent over Jeremy and pulled him by the arms out of the darkroom, through the hall, to the front door. Clare took one of his arms and pulled with me and we got him outside. I shut the door and knelt on the ground. My chest hurt as I breathed the clean air.

Clare had called a neighbour and he began to breathe into Jeremy, mouth to mouth.

'I called the ambulance,' Clare said, 'but they say that there's no gas in Lambourn.'

'It's hydrogen sulphide. A deadly gas.'

I breathed painfully and felt ill from the gas. Jeremy didn't move. Jeremy, don't die. Jeremy, it's my fault. Why hadn't I burned George Millace's rubbish?

The ambulance arrived, and a police car, and Harold, and a doctor, and half of Lambourn. The doctor looked at Jeremy and they lifted him into the ambulance. They shut the doors and drove him to Swindon.

Don't die, Jeremy. It's my fault.

'Jeremy, don't die. Jeremy, it's my fault.'

The fire engine arrived. The men went into my house with masks over their faces. They carried a machine which could measure the gas. When they came out, they shook their heads.

'No one must enter the house until the gas has disappeared.'

'Where did the gas come from?' the police inspector asked me.

I shook my head. 'I don't know.'

'What's wrong with your face?'

'I fell in a race,' I explained. He accepted it. Injured jockeys were often seen in Lambourn.

'How did you know that the gas was dangerous?' he asked.

'Sulphide is sometimes used for developing photographs. I've smelt it before, but I didn't have any.'

The inspector left. 'I'll be back in the morning.'

Clare returned to London and I went to stay with Harold. The next morning the police inspector appeared again.

'There's a water filter on the tap in your darkroom,' he said. 'What do you use it for?'

'All water for photographs must be clean,' I said. 'The salt in the filter cleans the water.' My eyes, my mouth, were beginning to feel better.

'Your water filter contains sulphide. Not salt. And when the tap was turned on, out came the gas. So it wasn't an accident, sir.'

'But I use that tap all the time. I put salt in the water filter only recently.'

'Who knew you had a water filter?'

'Everyone with a darkroom has a filter.'

The inspector was silent. Who had tried to kill me with gas? Den Relgan had beaten me. Had he used gas, too? Perhaps someone else wanted to kill me. Perhaps Dana den Relgan's list was in George Millace's box.

'No one's been in my house since Wednesday, when I used the darkroom. Only my neighbour, and the man from the water company . . .'

'What man?'

'Ask my neighbour. She saw him. She said that he wanted to check the pipes.'

The inspector stood up. 'I'll talk to her now.'

'What about Jeremy?'

'He's still alive.'

I went back to my house. The police had searched it, but George's box was still on the table in the kitchen. The black envelope was still there, with the piece of clear plastic.

I had to find out what it was . . . and fast.

14

Hidden list

The hospital phoned. Jeremy was awake. He was still very ill, but he was not going to die. I phoned Clare and told her.

'Can I come and stay with you? Until Saturday?' I asked.

'Why not? Come tonight.'

I told Harold that I would be well enough to race on Saturday. I packed a bag, picked up George's box, and drove to London. Samantha and Clare stared at my face. Black and purple and yellow bruises.

'But it's worse!' Clare said.

'It looks worse, but feels better,' I said. In fact, my whole body was covered with similar bruises.

Samantha was worried. 'Clare said that someone had hit you . . . but I never thought . . .'

'Look,' I said, 'I could go somewhere else.'

'Of course not. Sit down. Supper's ready.'

For two days I slept and waited to feel better. On Wednesday Samantha asked me, 'Who hit you?'

I didn't answer. Her house felt like home, and she had been welcoming and friendly to me after all those years. But I wasn't used to talking about my troubles. I had been on my own for too long. Samantha didn't ask again, but I knew that she was hurt. Clare came home from work and she too, though she did not ask, was waiting.

During supper, I began to talk. I told them all about George Millace. I didn't decide to tell them; it just happened naturally. They listened as they ate slowly.

'I carried on what George had begun,' I said. 'It isn't finished yet. I didn't feel safe at my house. I'm not going back there until I know who tried to kill me.'

On Friday my face looked better. I drove north out of London to Basildon in Essex, to a factory which made paper for printing photographs.

'Do you make any paper which looks like plastic?' I asked in the front office.

They did not. Had I brought the paper with me?

'No,' I said. 'I was afraid to bring it into the light. Could I see someone else?'

Difficult, they said.

I waited.

Perhaps Mr Christopher could help me, they said at last, if he wasn't too busy.

Mr Christopher was about nineteen years old. I described the plastic and the paper to him. He shook his head.

I tried another question. 'Why would a photographer want ammonia?'

Mr Christopher stared. 'Only in order to print on diazo paper. It's used to print drawings. The drawing disappears under a bright light, and the diazo paper is then developed in hot ammonia.'

'What does diazo paper look like?'

'It looks just like paper. Diazo film looks like plastic.'

'How can I develop diazo film?'

'Easily,' Mr Christopher said. 'Put cold ammonia on the piece of plastic, then take it into light. The lines of the drawing will appear. Not too much light. In sunlight, thirty seconds.'

'And the paper?' I asked. 'It's white on both sides.'

'Heat some ammonia in a pan and hold the paper over the top. Don't get it wet. Just hold it above the ammonia.'

'Would you', I said carefully, 'like some champagne for lunch?'

I returned to Samantha's house at about six o'clock with a cheap pan and two bottles of ammonia. I was very tired and I hoped I would be well enough to ride tomorrow. Samantha had gone out and Clare was working on the table in the kitchen, her dark head bent over her book.

She looked up at me. 'A drink?' she asked.

I got us both a drink and sat at the table. I began to feel better. I fetched George's box of rubbish and took the piece of plastic from the black envelope. I put it on a plate and put some ammonia on it. Immediately, dark red writing began to appear. I put more ammonia on it, turned it over, and there was Dana's list.

Names, dates, drugs. The list Dana had written on the cigarette packet.

Clare looked up from her work. 'What have you found?'

'What Dana wanted.'

She came across the room and looked at the plate. 'That's a dangerous list. How did you find it?'

I told her about Mr Christopher in Basildon. 'George Millace was an extraordinary man,' I said.

'Extraordinary.' Clare looked at me. 'Perhaps all photographers are extraordinary.'

I accepted the word without thinking. A photographer. Not a jockey.

I opened the windows. Then I put more ammonia into the pan and began to heat it on the cooker. I held the piece of paper over the pan and watched George's letter appear.

The letter was written to someone I knew. When I read the name, I knew who had killed George.

And I could guess who wanted me to die.

*I held the piece of paper over the pan and watched
George's letter appear.*

Victor talks

Harold met me outside the weighing room at Sandown on Saturday.

'You look better. Have you seen the doctor?'

'He signed my card.'

'Victor's here,' Harold said. 'He doesn't want to talk to you here. He's coming to Lambourn on Monday and he'll talk to you then. And, Philip, be careful what you say.'

'Mmm,' I said. 'How about the horse today? Is Coral Key running to win?'

'Victor said nothing.'

'Then I'm riding to win.'

Steve Millace was in the weighing room. He was annoyed because he had ridden in last. But his mother was much better.

Lord White was outside. He looked at me quickly and then looked away. He would never be comfortable with me.

Victor Briggs was waiting with the horse. Coral Key was a good horse, a young horse who could run well. Victor said nothing. He watched me and kept his mouth shut.

The race began. Coral Key started well. He jumped the

first two fences, then up the hill, round the top bend. Then downhill, to the next seven fences. We were in second place then, but Coral Key began to tire as we ran up the hill – and the other horse won.

Harold said, 'He ran well.'

Victor Briggs said nothing.

I won my second race, but the horse didn't belong to Victor.

'Good race!' the owner said. 'You rode well!'

Victor Briggs watched, and said nothing.

Clare and I went to see Jeremy. He was lying, thinner than ever, his face grey, in a hospital bed.

'I'm sorry,' I said. 'It was my fault.'

'Don't forget I was there because I wanted to be.' He looked carefully at me. 'Your face looks OK. You got better fast.'

'How long will you be in here?'

'Three or four days. I'm breathing much better. That gas was so quick. I had no time to do anything.'

We were silent.

Clare said, 'A gas like that would kill somebody immediately – if they were alone in the house.'

On Sunday, I went to Lambourn. My house was cold and it no longer felt like home. The person who had lived there was going away. I was changing.

I put several photographs of different people on the

table in the kitchen and then I asked my neighbour Mrs Jackson to come in and look at them.

'What am I looking for, Mr Nore?'

'Anyone you've seen before.'

She studied them carefully, one by one, and stopped at one face. 'How extraordinary!' she said. 'That's the man from the water company, the one who came here.'

'Are you sure?'

She didn't hesitate. 'Absolutely. He was wearing the same hat, too.'

I gave her a pen. 'Please write on the back for me, Mrs Jackson, and sign your name.'

'Are you giving this to the police?' she asked. 'I don't want them round again, really. Will they come back again, with their questions?'

'I don't think so.'

Victor Briggs came in his Mercedes on Monday. He told me to get in the car and he drove up into the hills. He parked and turned off the engine.

'Do you know what I'm going to say?' I asked.

'I hear things,' he said. 'I heard about den Relgan. I heard that you got him out of the Jockey Club faster than he got in. I heard that he beat you.'

He watched my surprise.

'George Millace sent you a letter,' I said quietly.

He moved in his seat. 'How long have you had it?'

'Three weeks.'

'You can't use it. You'd be in trouble yourself.'

'How did you know that I had it?' I asked.

He said slowly, 'I heard that you had George Millace's papers, from Ivor. And Dana. Separately. Ivor said that you were worse than George.'

I thought about the letter.

Dear Victor

You will be interested in some information which I have about five of your horses. All five horses were ridden by Philip Nore. They were favourites but they didn't win their races. And you made a lot of money.

The Jockey Club would be interested in this information.

I will ring you soon, however, with another idea.

Yours sincerely

George Millace

The letter had been sent three years ago. For three years, Victor Briggs had allowed his horses to win. When George Millace died, Victor Briggs went back to the old game.

'I didn't want to do anything about the letter,' I said.

Victor stared at me. 'Yesterday I added up my money,' he said. 'I've made more money since you began to ride honest races, than I made when you lost races on my orders. I know that you've changed. You're a different person. Older. Stronger. I won't ask you again to lose a race.' He stopped. 'Is that enough? Is that what you want to hear?'

I looked away, across the windy hills. 'Yes.'

We were silent. After a while, Victor said, 'George Millace didn't ask for money, you know. At least . . .'

'The Injured Jockeys Fund?'

'You know everything, don't you?'

'I've learned.'

Victor drove away and I walked back over the hills to Lambourn. I thought about the past weeks. I thought about Samantha and Clare, about Jeremy. People I cared about. I looked down at Lambourn. I saw Harold's house and stables, the row of houses with mine in the centre. It had been my home for seven years. But now I was ready to leave.

I would race, I thought, until the end of the season. Five or six more months. Then, in May or June, when summer came, I would put away my boots and stop racing.

I was ready to move on, to live in another house. To marry Clare . . . I would be a photographer.

I went on down the hill.

'You know everything, don't you?' said Victor.

16

The last photographs

Clare came down on the train two days later to collect some of my photographs. She was going to get work for me. I laughed. It was serious, she said.

I had no races that day. We were going to fetch Jeremy from the hospital and take him home. I phoned Lance Kinship and told him I had the copies of his photographs. Could I bring them to his house that afternoon? Fine, he said.

Jeremy looked much better. He sat in the back of the car and we drove to Lance Kinship's house.

'Sorry about this,' I said. 'But it won't take long.'

They didn't mind.

It was a large house, with big gates. I picked up the packet of photographs and rang the front door bell.

'Come inside,' Kinship said. 'I'll pay you.'

'OK. I must be quick, though. My friends are waiting.'

He looked at the car where Clare and Jeremy were sitting. We went into a large sitting room, with black furniture and glass tables. I gave him the packet of photographs.

'Look at them,' I said.

He pulled out the photographs. The top photograph showed him wearing his hat.

'Turn it over,' I said.

He turned it over and read what Mrs Jackson had written: 'This is the man from the water company . . .'

His face changed.

'Before you say anything,' I said, 'look at the other photographs.'

He looked at them – Dana's list, and the letter which I had found on the diazo paper. With angry fingers he dropped the photographs on the floor.

'She said that you didn't have the list . . . She said that you knew nothing . . .'

'You can see your name on her list.'

'I'll kill you,' he said.

'No, you won't. It's too late now. The gas didn't kill me.'

He said, 'It all went wrong. But I thought that it didn't matter, because you didn't have the list.'

'But I do have the list, and George's letter. And a copy of the letter is in an envelope in my bank. The bank will open the envelope if I die.'

Lance looked at the photographs on the floor. 'George's letter . . .' he said.

'When George telephoned you,' I asked, 'did he tell you his "other idea"?'

Lance Kinship began to grow angry. 'I'm telling you nothing.'

'Did George tell you to give money to the Injured Jockeys Fund? Did he tell you when he stopped here for a drink?'

Lance Kinship was silent.

'Did you put something into his whisky?'

'Prove it!' Kinship shouted.

I couldn't prove it, of course. 'I'm here now,' I said, 'not George. And I'm not asking for money.'

He stared at me.

'My mother died from drugs,' I told him.

He said wildly, 'But I didn't know your mother!'

'No, of course you didn't. But I don't like people who sell drugs.'

He stepped towards me. I thought that he was going to fight; but he stepped on one of the photographs and fell on to one knee. He looked up at me and I saw no anger, only fear.

I said, 'I don't want money. I want you to tell me who sells the drugs to you.'

Slowly he stood up. 'I can't. I can't!'

'It can't be difficult,' I said quietly. 'You must know where you buy them.'

'You don't know . . .' Kinship was breathing with difficulty. 'I can't tell you. I'd be . . . dead.'

I shook my head. 'No one will know. I'm not going to tell anyone *your* name, but the name that you give me will go to the drugs police.'

'I can't,' he said desperately.

'If you don't,' I said, 'I'll tell the police about the man from the water company. First.'

He was trembling.

'Tell me the name,' I said. 'Of course, I expect you'll have to find a new contact then. So in a year or two, I'll ask you for another name.'

His face was grey. 'It will go on?'

'That's right. You killed George Millace. You tried to kill me. You nearly killed my friend.' I took out a notebook and a pen. 'Write now,' I said.

He sat down and wrote a name and address.

'And sign it.'

'Sign?'

'Of course. Your name.'

He wrote: Lance Kinship.

I picked up the notebook and put it in my pocket. I would photograph it and keep the negative safe.

'That's all,' I said. 'For now.'

He didn't move.

I went outside and paused in the winter air. When George Millace was alive, I hadn't liked him. But now, I felt close to him. I had discovered his secrets, I knew his plans. I had fired his guns.

I got into the car.

'Everything all right?' Clare asked.

'Yes,' I said.

GLOSSARY

ammonia a gas or liquid with a sharp smell

anger the strong feeling that makes people angry

blackmail asking for money from somebody in return for not
telling secret or criminal information about them

champagne an expensive alcoholic drink made from white grapes

chemical a liquid used to change another material

collar bone a bone which joins the shoulder and the chest

darkroom a room made dark so that photographs can be
developed

diazo a way of copying drawings

drug a harmful 'medicine' which can become a habit and make
you ill or kill you

ex-jockey a person who used to be a jockey

fence a wall made of wood

filter *(n)* something which cleans water as the water passes
through it

fire *(v)* to shoot with a gun

funeral a special event when a dead person is buried

gallop *(v)* (of a horse) to go at the fastest speed

give up to stop doing or trying to do something

helmet a hard hat that keeps the head safe

hydrogen sulphide a gas with a smell like bad eggs

insure to pay a little money regularly to a company so that it
will give you a lot of money if you have an accident

jockey a person who rides horses in races

lord a man who is the head of an important family

mask *(n)* a cover for the face so that the person cannot be
recognized

mind *(n)* the part of a person which thinks, feels and remembers

negative a film which shows dark as light, and light as dark

plastic a light, strong material made in factories and used for making many useful things

print *(v)* to use a machine to make words or pictures on paper

print *(n)* a photograph printed on paper

professional doing something as a job, not as a hobby

publisher someone who makes books to sell

race *(v)* to try to go faster than others

race *(n)* a test of speed

safe *(n)* a strong cupboard in which money and valuable things are kept safely

stable a building where horses are kept

tap *(n)* a pipe for water which can be opened or closed

weighing room a room where the heaviness of jockeys is measured before each race

Reflex

ACTIVITIES

Before Reading

1 **Read the story introduction on the first page of the book, and the back cover. How much do you know now about the story? Are these sentences true (T) or false (F)?**

1 George Millace gives Philip his photographic secrets before he dies. T/F

2 Philip doesn't like losing races. T/F

3 Everyone wants to destroy George's photographs except Philip. T/F

4 Philip can uncover George's secrets because he knows a lot about horses. T/F

5 Horse-racing is a fast and sometimes dangerous sport. T/F

6 George Millace died in a mysterious way. T/F

7 Philip is the only person who knows about George's secret photographs. T/F

2 **Can you guess what will happen in this story? Choose answers to these questions (you can choose more than one).**

1 What will Philip do with George's secrets? He will . . .

a) tell his friends about them.

b) tell nobody about them.

c) get money for them.

d) destroy them.

2 What will happen to Philip himself? He will . . .

a) be beaten up by someone.

b) give up riding in races.

c) give up photography.

d) fall in love.

While Reading

Read Chapters 1 to 5, and then answer these questions.

1 Why was Philip angry when he was told to lose the race?
2 What was the reason for George Millace's crash?
3 Why did Philip want the box of photographic rubbish?
4 How did Victor try to thank Philip for losing the race?
5 Why was the photo of Yaxley and O'Tree important?
6 How was Ivor den Relgan different from other Jockey Club members?
7 Why did Philip feel safe with George's secrets?
8 How did Dana know Lance, and why did Ivor hit him?
9 Why did Jeremy advise Philip to destroy the photos?

Before you read Chapter 6, can you guess the answers to these questions?

1 Who are the man and the woman in George's photo?
   a) Ivor den Relgan and Lady White
   b) Lord White and Dana den Relgan
   c) Ivor den Relgan and Dana den Relgan
   d) Lance Kinship and Lady White
   e) Lance Kinship and Dana den Relgan
2 Why did George drive his car into a tree?
   a) Because he had drunk too much whisky and fell asleep.
   b) Because someone had put something in his whisky.

Read Chapters 6 to 9. Choose the best question-word for these questions, and then answer them.

How / What / Why

1 . . . did Philip refuse to cheat on Daylight?
2 . . . had Philip first met Samantha?
3 . . . did Lance Kinship ask Philip to take photos of him?
4 . . . did Philip feel about Clare's interest in his photos?
5 . . . was making Lady White unhappy?
6 . . . did the races on Daylight and Chainmail go?
7 . . . did Philip learn from Mrs Millace about George's journey home from Doncaster?
8 . . . was Philip surprised at seeing Elgin Yaxley?
9 . . . was the Injured Jockeys Fund for?

Before you read Chapter 10, can you guess what George's 'other idea' is in his blackmail letters?

1 Paying George a lot of money.
2 Paying somebody else a lot of money.
3 Paying George some money every month for the rest of his life.
4 Buying George a racehorse and paying for its training.

Read Chapters 10 to 13. Who said this, and to whom? Who, or what, were they talking about?

1 'They say that cameras do lie.'
2 'They had an emergency meeting of the Jockey Club in London this morning. He's out.'

3 'George said only once . . . and now *you*!'

4 'He showed me his papers, and I came in with him.'

5 'Burnt! To the ground!'

6 'Someone's done this to you, haven't they?'

7 'You have got it, haven't you?'

8 'It wasn't an accident, sir.'

Before you read Chapter 14, can you guess what happens? Choose endings for these sentences.

1 Philip finds the secret on the clear plastic and . . .

    a) goes to the police.   c) goes to see George's killer.

    b) destroys it.   d) talks to a newspaper.

2 The man from the water company was . . .

    a) Ivor den Relgan.   c) Elgin Yaxley.

    b) Lance Kinship.   d) Victor Briggs.

Read Chapters 14 to 16. Rewrite this incorrect summary with the correct information.

On the diazo film and paper Philip discovered a list of names of racehorses, and a letter written by Ivor den Relgan to Dana. Because of this letter, he knew that nobody had killed George. Philip's mother had died in an accident, so Philip planned to make Victor Briggs give him the names of jockeys who lost races. He would then give these names to the Jockey Club.

Victor Briggs told Philip he would continue to ask him to lose races. However, Philip decided to become a racehorse trainer, stay in Lambourn, and marry Clare.

After Reading

1 **What did Philip tell Samantha and Clare (see page 74)? Put the parts of sentences in the right order, and join them with these linking words to make a paragraph of six sentences. Begin with number 5.**

and / because / but / but / so / when / where / which / who

1 Yaxley had told the police he'd never met the man

2 _____ proved that Dana was not Ivor's daughter.

3 You don't make money if your horse loses a race,

4 _____ he took secret photographs of them

5 Three years ago, George Millace found out that Victor Briggs was making a lot of money

6 _____ shot his horses,

7 to make them pay money to the Injured Jockeys Fund.

8 _____ George knew that Briggs was cheating.

9 George kept all these people's secrets,

10 _____ Yaxley received a lot of money from the insurers.

11 _____ George knew that Yaxley was lying

12 Then, last summer, George saw Ivor den Relgan with his daughter Dana in St Tropez,

13 _____ he wrote blackmail letters to them all,

14 A year later, Elgin Yaxley's five horses were shot dead,

15 _____ he'd taken a photo of Yaxley talking to this man in a café in France.

16 _____ the horses he owned lost their races.

2 **Perhaps this is what some of the characters in the story were thinking. Which six characters are they, and what is happening, or has just happened, in the story?**

1 'I thought she was a really sweet girl, and all the time . . . I suppose she and her so-called father planned it together. Well, he's going to get a nasty surprise, because I'm going to ring the Secretary of the Jockey Club right now . . .'

2 'I don't have any luck. He's worse than Millace – just standing there and staring at me with those cold eyes. Seven and a half thousand! And where am I going to go this time? It doesn't have to be Hong Kong, anyway . . .'

3 'Well . . . I'm alive, I think. I wonder if I can move anything . . . Ouch! Stupid idea. Perhaps I'm dying. That would be nice. I'll just lie here and see . . .'

4 'Well, that's over. I think I'm safe. I've told him what he wants to hear. He can't use the letter against me, because it would make trouble for him too. And I'll let him ride how he wants in future – it's better for both of us that way.'

5 'Oh no, there's blood all over my coat too. Stupid man! He thinks he's so clever, so tough! But he's not going to stop me – I'll see her at the next party, anyway . . .'

6 'What will I do if Ivor's killed him? Please, please let him be alive! I've got to get it back. Lance will kill me if I don't. Or Ivor will. Oh please, answer the door! Yes – somebody's coming . . .'

3 **What did Harold say to Victor Briggs about Philip before the races at Ascot? (See pages 31 and 43.) Complete their conversation (use as many words as you like).**

VICTOR: Harold? Briggs here. I want to talk about Nore.
HAROLD: _____
VICTOR: Ride to win? Harold, *I* give the orders, not him.
    What's the matter with him? He's cheated before.
HAROLD: _____
Victor: I know he's a good horse, Harold, and OK, Nore's a
    good jockey. So what?
HAROLD: _____
VICTOR: He could be right, I suppose. What do you think?
HAROLD: _____
VICTOR: Well, perhaps you're right, Harold. OK, you can tell
    him I've changed my mind. But he'd better win!

4 **Before he went to see Lance Kinship, Philip left a letter at his bank. Complete it by choosing the best word for each gap.**

George Millace kept a box of _____ 'rubbish', and after his
death I discovered this was Millace's way of _____ secret
_____ and letters. He was using these secrets to _____ people.
Among these things was a _____ of people who sold _____ at
parties. One of these people was Lance Kinship, who I believe
_____ George Millace by _____ something in his whisky,
which caused Millace to _____ his car. I have no _____ of
this, but I can _____ that Kinship tried to kill me. My
neighbour _____ him as the 'man from the water company'
who put hydrogen sulphide in the water _____ in my _____.

I plan to make Kinship give me the _____ of his contacts in the drugs world, which I will give to the _____. If I suddenly _____ or disappear, please give them this letter at once.

5 **Match these halves of sentences to make five 'blackmailing' sentences, used by George Millace. For each sentence, say who George was speaking or writing to.**

1 If you don't want me to tell the police about you and the drugs you sell,

2 I won't show the photo of you and Ivor to Lord White.

3 Unless you give a thousand pounds to the Injured Jockeys Fund,

4 this photo of you and your friend in France will be in the hands of the police tomorrow.

5 The Jockey Club will hear about the money you made when your horses lost,

6 you'll have to listen to another idea of mine.

7 If you write me a list of names, dates and drugs,

8 I'll tell Lord White that Dana is not your daughter.

9 if you don't give some of it to the Injured Jockeys Fund.

10 Unless you leave Britain and go and live in Hong Kong,

6 **Do you agree (A) or disagree (D) with these sentences? Explain why.**

1 Philip was wrong to continue with George's blackmail.

2 Lance's crimes were the worst, because one person died and another was nearly killed.

3 Blackmail is not bad if it stops other crimes.

ABOUT THE AUTHOR

Dick Francis was born in South Wales in 1920. He can't remember learning to ride – it came to him as naturally as learning to walk, and as a boy he won many awards at horse shows. After six years in the Royal Air Force during the Second World War he became a jockey, and in the 1953–54 season he was Champion Jockey, winning seventy-six races. He rode eight times in the famous Grand National Steeplechase and in 1956 he was close to winning when his horse, which was well in front, slipped up just forty metres from the winning post. Francis called this 'both the high point and the low point' of his life as a jockey. He and his wife Mary now live in the Cayman Islands, in the British West Indies.

Dick Francis published his first thriller, *Dead Cert*, in 1962, and there has been a bestseller every year since (his fortieth title is *Second Wind*). His novels *Forfeit* (1968), *Whip Hand* (1979) and *Come to Grief* (1995) have won Edgar Allan Poe Awards from the Mystery Writers of America, and he has also received Silver, Gold, and Diamond Dagger awards from the British Crime Writers Association. Francis is described as one of the world's finest thriller writers, and his books have been translated into more than thirty languages.

All his stories are carefully researched (his wife and two sons often help with this). They are told in the first person by heroes who, like Philip Nore in *Reflex*, are ordinary men, tested and changed by their experiences. The result is always a fast-moving, 'unputdownable' story. Once you have read one Dick Francis novel, you will want to read another – and another!

OXFORD BOOKWORMS LIBRARY

Classics • Crime & Mystery • Factfiles • Fantasy & Horror
Human Interest • Playscripts • Thriller & Adventure
True Stories • World Stories

The OXFORD BOOKWORMS LIBRARY provides enjoyable reading in English, with a wide range of classic and modern fiction, non-fiction, and plays. It includes original and adapted texts in seven carefully graded language stages, which take learners from beginner to advanced level. An overview is given on the next pages.

All Stage 1 titles are available as audio recordings, as well as over eighty other titles from Starter to Stage 6. All Starters and many titles at Stages 1 to 4 are specially recommended for younger learners. Every Bookworm is illustrated, and Starters and Factfiles have full-colour illustrations.

The OXFORD BOOKWORMS LIBRARY also offers extensive support. Each book contains an introduction to the story, notes about the author, a glossary, and activities. Additional resources include tests and worksheets, and answers for these and for the activities in the books. There is advice on running a class library, using audio recordings, and the many ways of using Oxford Bookworms in reading programmes. Resource materials are available on the website <www.oup.com/bookworms>.

The *Oxford Bookworms Collection* is a series for advanced learners. It consists of volumes of short stories by well-known authors, both classic and modern. Texts are not abridged or adapted in any way, but carefully selected to be accessible to the advanced student.

You can find details and a full list of titles in the *Oxford Bookworms Library Catalogue* and *Oxford English Language Teaching Catalogues*, and on the website <www.oup.com/bookworms>.

THE OXFORD BOOKWORMS LIBRARY
GRADING AND SAMPLE EXTRACTS

STARTER • 250 HEADWORDS

present simple – present continuous – imperative –
can/cannot, must – *going to* (future) – simple gerunds ...

Her phone is ringing – but where is it?

Sally gets out of bed and looks in her bag. No phone. She looks under the bed. No phone. Then she looks behind the door. There is her phone. Sally picks up her phone and answers it. *Sally's Phone*

STAGE 1 • 400 HEADWORDS

... past simple – coordination with *and*, *but*, *or* –
subordination with *before*, *after*, *when*, *because*, *so* ...

I knew him in Persia. He was a famous builder and I worked with him there. For a time I was his friend, but not for long. When he came to Paris, I came after him – I wanted to watch him. He was a very clever, very dangerous man. *The Phantom of the Opera*

STAGE 2 • 700 HEADWORDS

... present perfect – *will* (future) – *(don't) have to, must not, could* –
comparison of adjectives – simple *if* clauses – past continuous –
tag questions – *ask/tell* + infinitive ...

While I was writing these words in my diary, I decided what to do. I must try to escape. I shall try to get down the wall outside. The window is high above the ground, but I have to try. I shall take some of the gold with me – if I escape, perhaps it will be helpful later. *Dracula*

... should, may – present perfect continuous – *used to* – past perfect –
causative – relative clauses – indirect statements ...

Of course, it was most important that no one should see
Colin, Mary, or Dickon entering the secret garden. So Colin
gave orders to the gardeners that they must all keep away
from that part of the garden in future. **The Secret Garden**

STAGE 4 • 1400 HEADWORDS
... past perfect continuous – passive (simple forms) –
would conditional clauses – indirect questions –
relatives with *where/when* – gerunds after prepositions/phrases ...

I was glad. Now Hyde could not show his face to the world
again. If he did, every honest man in London would be proud
to report him to the police. **Dr Jekyll and Mr Hyde**

STAGE 5 • 1800 HEADWORDS
... future continuous – future perfect –
passive (modals, continuous forms)
would have conditional clauses – modals + perfect infinitive ...

If he had spoken Estella's name, I would have hit him. I was so
angry with him, and so depressed about my future, that I could
not eat the breakfast. Instead I went straight to the old house.
Great Expectations

STAGE 6 • 2500 HEADWORDS
... passive (infinitives, gerunds) – advanced modal meanings –
clauses of concession, condition

When I stepped up to the piano, I was confident. It was as if I
knew that the prodigy side of me really did exist. And when I
started to play, I was so caught up in how lovely I looked that
I didn't worry how I would sound. **The Joy Luck Club**

The Thirty-Nine Steps

JOHN BUCHAN

Retold by Nick Bullard

'I turned on the light, but there was nobody there. Then I saw something in the corner that made my blood turn cold. Scudder was lying on his back. There was a long knife through his heart, pinning him to the floor.'

Soon Richard Hannay is running for his life across the hills of Scotland. The police are chasing him for a murder he did not do, and another, more dangerous enemy is chasing him as well – the mysterious 'Black Stone'. Who are these people? And why do they want Hannay dead?

The Big Sleep

RAYMOND CHANDLER

Retold by Rosalie Kerr

General Sternwood has four million dollars, and two young daughters, both pretty and both wild. He's an old, sick man, close to death, but he doesn't like being blackmailed. So he asks private detective Philip Marlowe to get the blackmailer off his back.

Marlowe knows the dark side of life in Los Angeles well, and nothing much surprises him. But the Sternwood girls are a lot wilder than their old father realizes. They like men, drink, drugs – and it's not just a question of blackmail.